Small Fires, Little Flames

poems by

Adam Penna

Finishing Line Press
Georgetown, Kentucky

Small Fires, Little Flames

Copyright © 2017 by Adam Penna
ISBN 978-1-63534-293-2 First Edition
All rights reserved under International and Pan-American Copyright Conventions.
No part of this book may be reproduced in any manner whatsoever without written permission from the publisher, except in the case of brief quotations embodied in critical articles and reviews.

ACKNOWLEDGMENTS

4 (The blue jay opens like a rusty hinge) first appeared in *The Long Islander* as "The World at 8 AM."

Publisher: Leah Maines

Editor: Christen Kincaid

Cover Art: Max Stablein

Author Photo: Max Stablein

Cover Design: Elizabeth Maines McCleavy

Printed in the USA on acid-free paper.
Order online: www.finishinglinepress.com
also available on amazon.com

Author inquiries and mail orders:
Finishing Line Press
P. O. Box 1626
Georgetown, Kentucky 40324
U. S. A.

Table of Contents

1 (Could I have felt those things?)
2 (I don't know what a dream is)
3 (I did at last go underground)
4 (The blue jay opens like a rusty hinge)
5 (It's hard for them to be alone)
6 (Children, trying to stay awake)
7 (Now it's morning quiet, and it's cool)
8 (These leaves hope more than I do now)
9 (The flowers stand in a vase)
10 (If there was a light)
11 (The light and the cool air)
12 (The page, like the field, lies here)
13 (I went to watch the painful buds)
14 (Happiness barks because her master left)
15 (Clarity comes and then)
16 (It happens that a word or two)
17 (Always the stars are in error)
18 (The magician learns his art)
19 (What god would prick)
20 (*I would revise so much*)
21 (What word was it? Oh, yes)
22 (Happiness is *realize*)
23 (After my wife and the cats have gone to sleep)
24 (When I was a saint I knew)
25 (I see an answered prayer)
26 (Small prayers for small gods)
27 (A chip means: *birds, birds, birds*)
28 (The stars convince us: *Wish*)
29 (Wish on a shooting star)
30 (I used to think courage)

For Shannon, my rescue

1

Could I have felt those things?
I said them. I wrote them down.
They are the best parts of my life.

The pages like a catalogue of sins.
Here, I have been too sad.
There, I might have given more.

Celebration comes at the end,
when, after stumbling a long time, finally,
we fall. The rest is lying in the grass.

2

I don't know what a dream is.
I've never entered into one

and failed to change some fact,
which now I'm sure is all there is

of truth. My life is like a dream.
I don't know anything about it.

My death will be the first real thing
I won't obscure, refute or try to.

3

I did at last go underground.
It was night and the crickets sang.
It takes long mourning to recover
not what you lost but something else.

Perhaps it's better than you thought.
Perhaps it's not. You must make do.
Or everywhere you turn the world
will seem an evil place and people

will want to know what happened to
the man they used to know and love.
It's fair to say, *That stranger moved,*
but cruel to say, *He might come back.*

4

The blue jay opens like a rusty hinge.
It used to be I could be sure his song
was his. It used to be I knew his name.
But now I doubt, a little bit, enough.

It's good, I think, and makes me what my mother
dreamed I might be: a pair of ears and eyes.
And now the wind runs its hand through the leaves.
I hear it first before I turn my head.

I recognize: *There, there*. It takes all day
to catalogue the world at 8 AM
and a year more to capture 8:01.
Old men believe in take-your-time.

And that's because they hope to live as long
as there are things left in the world to name.
But I might let the afternoon fly by
without a single mark made on the page.

5

It's hard for them to be alone.
Soon she will be the earth, oblivion.
And these and those, and him especially.
You know I want to live because,
however much it hurts, I breathe.

6

Children, trying to stay awake,
know what I mean and do
exactly as I do, as I have done,
been doing since the crib.

They fight to shake off drowsiness
and cry because it hurts.
And, yes, they feel betrayed.
Even their mothers want to put them down

and do, with one hand pressed,
like gentleness, heavy on the chest,
then song sweet as a lullaby,
and finally the dark.

7

Now it's morning quiet, and it's cool.
A fan whirs somewhere in the house
and makes me think of birds:
of egrets, herons, ospreys, hawks,
and ordinary gulls as still as decoys on the waves.

Inside there is another buzz.
I've known its name, its species, and forgot.
Where does it burrow, when I wake?
Why does it surface, if not to sing,
like this bird now that says, I*'m here!*

8

These leaves hope more than I do now.
That's for the good.
I know it's hard for you to understand,
but listen close. The sound
means everything is as it is.
What sunshine can I hope for,
who's heading underground?
I know I know. And you do too

9

The flowers stand in a vase.
The sun has disappeared again.
The trees begin a steady crawl
to where I sit to watch them come.

10

If there was a light,
I couldn't see it.

I was awake. I'm sure.
But certainty would mean

it couldn't happen.
It did. And afterward

we ate delicious plates
of macaroni, gravy, pig.

We laughed and everyone
seemed doubled by the light.

11

The light and the cool air
are everywhere.

The birds feel too content
to sing. Today,

I take their part,
and sing a little and

this song sounds like the others
but better. Still,

the trees are what they are.
They never complain.

The other lessons weren't right.
They weren't wrong.

Tomorrow, this line begins.
It ends today.

12

The page, like the field, lies here.
The birds appear and disappear.
Their love waits in the trees.
It broods. What can we do but meet it there?
If I have dreamed a thousand times,
the wiregrass, the olive turned to sticks,
there was the snow to soften all,
and eyes, like mine but sharper, clear,
to frame the scene into a song. And I,
this week alone, despaired, because I did.
And died a little, too, and tried to live.

13

I went to watch the painful buds
break through the grey and silver bark.
I stayed all day to see a single leaf unfurl.
And somewhere else, close by, there was a beating heart
submerged and hopeful still, ready to rise.
If I had put my ear against the ground,
I might have heard and called it by its name.
I might have realized and stayed stiller, calm.

14

Happiness barks because her master left.
Where did he go?
Outside, the day releases.

When I get home my love will answer me.
This is the end of every story stars tell.
But here on earth,

our love begs for another chance to get it right. Defeat
is just another word for lightningstroke.
Or is it lightning*strike*?

The sky knows everything you might write in your book.
It anticipates destruction. Still, it doesn't care.
How could it and be so lovely, outrageous, far?

15

Clarity comes and then—
gone, just like that.
You knew it once,
confused, a child, yes.
You reached out first.
The dark was there.
It met your hands.
It was like swimming
before you knew how to.
Then you learned to cut through
what wanted to devour you.
Forget again, and lose.

16

It happens that a word or two,
the ordinary verbs and nouns,
sneak through the otherwise extravagant sounds.

God's voice is always simple, clear.
He says what you have known is best
is best and offers evidence to confirm the truth.

This is beyond learning by rote.
This is beyond spontaneous response.
This is a god calling creation good.

17

Always the stars are in error,
shining too late and dying before
they can be shaped into truth.

Let my life be like this, too.
And when I die, my children,
the wishing starts. So does the light.

18

The magician learns his art
and knows this spell or that
will turn a stone into a dove.
The audience participates and sees.
There was no bird and now there is.

And saints practice humility,
praying for God's will
who first caused doves to rise.
There is no art to this.
The congregation believes or disbelieves.

The poet is the one I love,
who tries to turn his heart into a dove
and fails or gets it right,
but no one cares or sees.

19

What god would prick
who could do more?

The one I know isn't a wind.
He is a whisper.

Among the many voices he is one,
advising yes and no.

So long to other notions of the divine!
This one must do.

It's been a good friend
since I was born.

20

I would revise so much
is how it used to go,
and then it changed and all
I used to know as loss
became not loss but possibility.
Potential is the better word.
I almost called it *hope*
but stopped, and would, just short
of that, because hope also means,
to my chagrin, hold on.

21

What word was it? Oh, yes.
That one the heron said.
Was it only yesterday I heard it?

Or the day before and all the rain…
It's better to be wet and know it
than think: *the sun, the sun.*

As if to pray were more than confirmation:
this is, and that's enough. No more
wishing for this monk. Yes, that's right.

22

Happiness is *realize*,
not loss returned.

Not what is gone come back.
No, and no, and no

are three things.
The bird waits in its nest.

It sings and it waits.
What it knows returns,

while what it wants flies.
The same song sounds different now.

Suddenly, the ground
looks like the sky.

And every branch between
another hook, a claw.

23

After my wife and the cats have gone to sleep,
the stars stand out a little brighter than before.
One loosens from the sky, and I know, *She is it.*

By morning the ordinary trees take shape.
I used to love them, too, when they were mothers.
Now they are only limbs and trunks and roots.

When I learn to dream again and that,
from here on out, all learning means remembering,
those stars will come to be just stars,

and that will be enough—the way it was,
when I first saw them, shimmering and cold,
and couldn't understand or fall asleep.

24

When I was a saint I knew
burying roadkill meant being a soul.
I made myself responsible. I spoke
the prayers I knew as best I could.
They were leaves only, browse and mold.
But still I understood. But still…

When I grew old, *my skin, my skin.*
The bark flaked back and the tree bled.
The sky is just the blank against
which hawks make circles, shadows, stains.
But underground a groundhog practices good faith.
Between men bless and lose and grieve.

25

I see an answered prayer.
It is a tree. I say, *Look, look—*
I made it all myself. I made it with my dream.

And so it was. And so it was with birds.
And the deer eat from my cupped hands.
O, emptiness; o, void; o, death inside!

Each word asks you to *come, devour me.*
If you can, you will; if you can't, I win.
Even our lullabies insist, *Wake up!*

26

Small prayers for small gods
mean small fires, little flames,
leaping from head to hand to mouth.
The page ignites and soon the book.
When I was a child I knew.
The trees in the backyard cower
because the wind will speak of flames.

27

A chip means: *birds, birds, birds.*
Sparrows are the last to hear the news.
But who will be the first, this year, to see?

28

The stars convince us: *Wish*.
I don't believe in promises.
But one proves true: the juncos
appear and disappear in the leaves.

29

Wish on a shooting star
but to an angel pray.
That prayer is easy. Say,
I'm here, which means,

I'm ready, and readiness
prepares a heart
to inch up to the precipice
and dive. The schemes

of scholars and rabbis
amount to this.
Saint Thomas turned
from Aristotle and learned

what reason fails to teach.
What can we do before
glory but kneel? Or faint
in ecstasy like Saint Teresa?

30

I used to think courage
meant going on no matter what
and then, because I read
biographies and some are smart,

I thought it meant *preferring*
to take an easier route,
but Persians block the way,
and that seemed right,

until I turned my back
on courage and principles,
and tried instead to be,
and then the leaves were leaves,

and the moon was just
a moon, and every day
was one more chance to see
more clearly than the day before.

Adam Penna is the author of two books of poetry, *Little Songs & Lyrics to Genji* (S4N Books, 2010) and *Love of a Sleeper* (Finishing Line Press, 2008). *Talk of Happiness*, a follow up to *Little Songs & Lyrics to Genji*, is forthcoming from S4N Books in late 2017.

Penna's work has appeared in many magazines and journals, including *Cimarron Review, Cider Press Review, Nimrod,* and *Verse Daily*. He has twice been nominated for a Pushcart Prize.

He lives in East Moriches, NY, with his family and is a professor of English at Suffolk County Community College. He keeps a blog at adampenna.com and is the former publisher and editor of the now defunct *Best Poem*.

www.ingramcontent.com/pod-product-compliance
Lightning Source LLC
LaVergne TN
LVHW041508070426
835507LV00012B/1419